Note to Parents
The **Lifesize Animal Counting Book** is an
ideal starting point for children who are
just beginning to investigate numbers.
Parents can devise counting games based
on the photographs, and pre-readers
can guess at the words by counting the
animals on each page. Children will learn
numbers from one to ten, 20, and 100 by
looking first at numerals, then at words,
while the photographs of familiar animals
turn learning about numbers into fun!

DK

A DORLING KINDERSLEY BOOK

Editor Djinn von Noorden
Designer Ingrid Mason
Assistant designer Susan St. Louis
Production Ruth Cobb

First American Edition, 1994
2 4 6 8 10 9 7 5 3 1
Published in the United States by
Dorling Kindersley Publishing, Inc.,
95 Madison Avenue, New York, New York 10016

Published in Great Britain by Dorling Kindersley Limited.
Distributed by Houghton Mifflin Company, Boston.

Library of Congress Cataloging-in-Publication Data

The Lifesize animal counting book.--1st American ed. p. cm.
ISBN 1-56458-517-4
1. Counting--Juvenile literature. 2. Animals--Juvenile literature.
[1. Counting. 2. Animals.]

QA113.L53 1994 513.2'11--dc20 [E] 93-33786 CIP AC

Color reproduction by Colourscan, Singapore.
Printed in Italy by L.E.G.O.

The • Lifesize

Animal Counting Book

DORLING KINDERSLEY
London • New York • Stuttgart

1
one

One greedy gorilla

2
two

Two contented cats

3
three

Three playful puppies

4
four

Four slow tortoises

5
five

Five wise owls

6
six

Six furry kittens

7
seven

Seven snuffly rabbits

8
eight

Three white ducks and five
fluffy ducklings
make eight.

9
nine

Nine nosy guinea pigs

23

10
ten

Nine cheeping chicks
and one fat hen
make
ten.

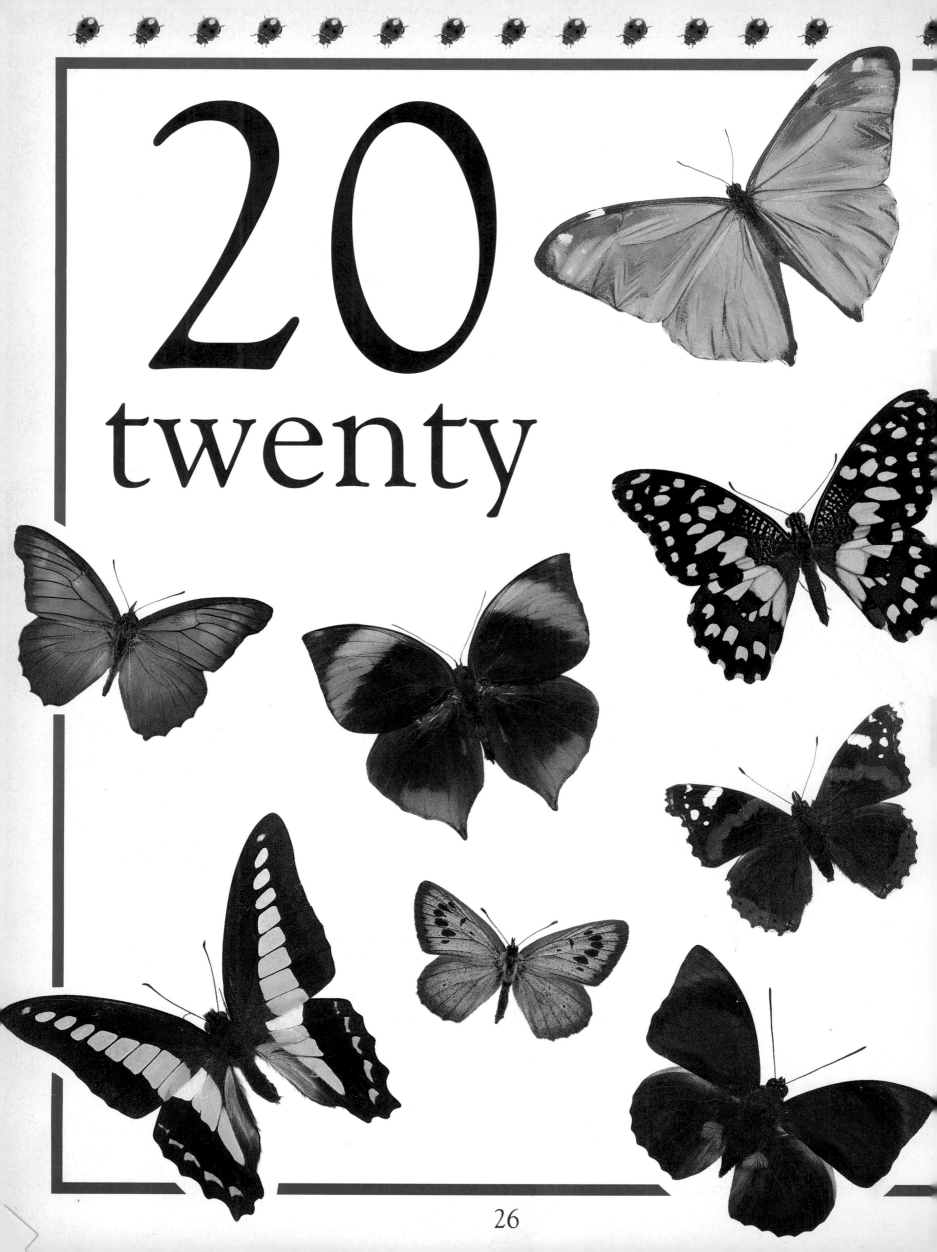

20
twenty

Twenty beautiful
butterflies

100
one
hundred

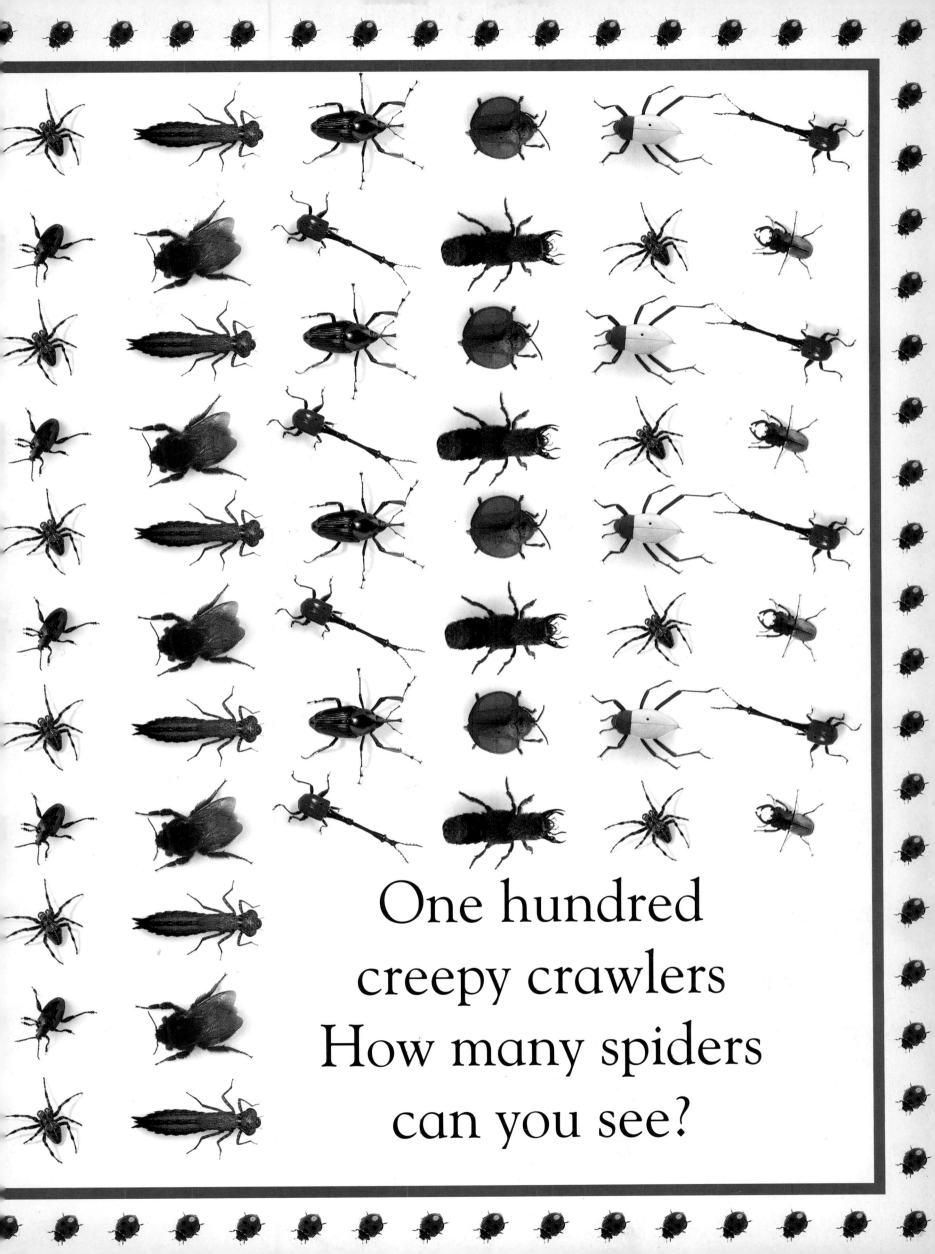

One hundred
creepy crawlers
How many spiders
can you see?